Guest book to celebrate

_____

_____

_____

_____

Happy thoughts......

_____

_____

_____

_____

_____

♥ *Love* _____

Happy thoughts......

_____

_____

_____

_____

_____

♥ *Love* _____

Happy thoughts......

_____

_____

_____

_____

_____

♥ *Love* _____

Happy thoughts......

_____

_____

_____

_____

_____

♥ *Love* _____

Happy thoughts......

_____

_____

_____

_____

_____

♥ *Love* _____

Happy thoughts......

_____

_____

_____

_____

_____

♥ *Love* _____

Happy thoughts......

_____

_____

_____

_____

_____

 Love _____

Happy thoughts......

_____

_____

_____

_____

_____

 Love _____

Happy thoughts......

♥ Love

Happy thoughts......

♥ Love

Happy thoughts......

_____

_____

_____

_____

_____

 Love
_____

Happy thoughts......

_____

_____

_____

_____

_____

 Love
_____

Happy thoughts......

♥ *Love*

Happy thoughts......

♥ *Love*

Happy thoughts......

_____

_____

_____

_____

_____

♥ *Love*

_____

Happy thoughts......

_____

_____

_____

_____

_____

♥ *Love*

_____

Happy thoughts......

_____

_____

_____

_____

_____

♥ *Love* _____

Happy thoughts......

_____

_____

_____

_____

_____

♥ *Love* _____

Happy thoughts......

_____

_____

_____

_____

♥ *Love* _____

Happy thoughts......

_____

_____

_____

_____

♥ *Love* _____

Happy thoughts......

♥ *Love*

Happy thoughts......

♥ *Love*

Happy thoughts......

_____

_____

_____

_____

_____

 Love

_____

Happy thoughts......

_____

_____

_____

_____

_____

 Love

_____

Happy thoughts......

_____

_____

_____

_____

_____

♥ Love_____

Happy thoughts......

_____

_____

_____

_____

_____

♥ Love_____

Happy thoughts......

_____

_____

_____

_____

_____

♥ *Love* _____

Happy thoughts......

_____

_____

_____

_____

_____

♥ *Love* _____

Happy thoughts......

_____

_____

_____

_____

_____

 Love

_____

Happy thoughts......

_____

_____

_____

_____

_____

Love

Happy thoughts......

_____

_____

_____

_____

_____

♥ *Love*

_____

Happy thoughts......

_____

_____

_____

_____

_____

♥ *Love*

Happy thoughts......

_____

_____

_____

_____

_____

♥ Love _____

Happy thoughts......

_____

_____

_____

_____

_____

♥ Love _____

Happy thoughts......

_____

_____

_____

_____

_____

♥ *Love*_____

Happy thoughts......

_____

_____

_____

_____

_____

♥ *Love*_____

Happy thoughts......

_____

_____

_____

_____

_____

♥ *Love*

_____

Happy thoughts......

_____

_____

_____

_____

_____

♥ *Love*

Happy thoughts......

_____

_____

_____

_____

_____

♥ *Love*
_____

Happy thoughts......

_____

_____

_____

_____

_____

♥ *Love*
_____

Happy thoughts......

_____

_____

_____

_____

_____

♥ *Love* _____

Happy thoughts......

_____

_____

_____

_____

_____

♥ *Love* _____

Happy thoughts......

_____

_____

_____

_____

_____

♥ *Love* _____

Happy thoughts......

_____

_____

_____

_____

_____

♥ *Love* _____

Happy thoughts......

_____

_____

_____

_____

_____

 Love

Happy thoughts......

_____

_____

_____

_____

_____

Love

Happy thoughts......

_____

_____

_____

_____

_____

♥ *Love* _____

Happy thoughts......

_____

_____

_____

_____

♥ *Love* _____

Happy thoughts......

_____

_____

_____

_____

_____

♥ *Love* _____

Happy thoughts......

_____

_____

_____

_____

_____

♥ *Love* _____

Happy thoughts......

_____

_____

_____

_____

_____

♥ Love
_____

Happy thoughts......

_____

_____

_____

_____

_____

♥ Love
_____

Happy thoughts......

 Love

Happy thoughts......

 Love

Happy thoughts......

♥ *Love*

Happy thoughts......

♥ *Love*

Happy thoughts......

_____

_____

_____

_____

_____

♥ *Love*
_____

Happy thoughts......

_____

_____

_____

_____

_____

♥ *Love*
_____

Happy thoughts......

_____

_____

_____

_____

_____

♥ *Love*
_____

Happy thoughts......

_____

_____

_____

_____

_____

♥ *Love*
_____

Happy thoughts......

_____

_____

_____

_____

♥ *Love* _____

Happy thoughts......

_____

_____

_____

_____

♥ *Love* _____

Happy thoughts......

_____

_____

_____

_____

_____

 Love

Happy thoughts......

_____

_____

_____

_____

_____

 Love

Happy thoughts......

_____

_____

_____

_____

_____

♥ *Love*

Happy thoughts......

_____

_____

_____

_____

_____

♥ *Love*

Happy thoughts......

♥ Love

Happy thoughts......

♥ Love

Happy thoughts......

_____

_____

_____

_____

_____

 Love _____

Happy thoughts......

_____

_____

_____

_____

_____

 Love _____

Happy thoughts......

_____

_____

_____

_____

_____

♥ *Love*
_____

Happy thoughts......

_____

_____

_____

_____

_____

♥ *Love*
_____

Happy thoughts......

_____

_____

_____

_____

_____

♥ *Love* _____

Happy thoughts......

_____

_____

_____

_____

_____

♥ *Love* _____

Happy thoughts......

_____

_____

_____

_____

♥ *Love*

Happy thoughts......

_____

_____

_____

_____

♥ *Love*

Happy thoughts......

_____

_____

_____

_____

_____

♥ *Love* _____

Happy thoughts......

_____

_____

_____

_____

_____

♥ *Love* _____

Happy thoughts......

_____

_____

_____

_____

_____

♥ *Love* _____

Happy thoughts......

_____

_____

_____

_____

_____

♥ *Love* _____

Happy thoughts......

_____

_____

_____

_____

_____

♥ Love _____

Happy thoughts......

_____

_____

_____

_____

_____

♥ Love _____

Happy thoughts......

_____

_____

_____

_____

_____

♥ *Love* _____

Happy thoughts......

_____

_____

_____

_____

_____

♥ *Love* _____

Happy thoughts......

_____

_____

_____

_____

_____

 Love _____

Happy thoughts......

_____

_____

_____

_____

_____

 Love _____

Happy thoughts......

_____

_____

_____

_____

_____

♥ Love

_____

Happy thoughts......

_____

_____

_____

_____

_____

♥ Love

Happy thoughts......

_____

_____

_____

_____

_____

♥ *Love*

Happy thoughts......

_____

_____

_____

_____

_____

♥ *Love*

Happy thoughts......

_____

_____

_____

_____

_____

 Love _____

Happy thoughts......

_____

_____

_____

_____

_____

 Love _____

Happy thoughts......

_____

_____

_____

_____

_____

 Love

_____

Happy thoughts......

_____

_____

_____

_____

_____

 Love

_____

Happy thoughts......

_____

_____

_____

_____

_____

♥ *Love* _____

Happy thoughts......

_____

_____

_____

_____

_____

♥ *Love* _____

Happy thoughts......

♥ *Love*

Happy thoughts......

♥ *Love*

Happy thoughts......

_____

_____

_____

_____

_____

♥ *Love* _____

Happy thoughts......

_____

_____

_____

_____

♥ *Love* _____

Happy thoughts......

_____

_____

_____

_____

_____

 Love

Happy thoughts......

_____

_____

_____

_____

_____

 Love

Happy thoughts......

_____

_____

_____

_____

_____

♥ *Love* _____

Happy thoughts......

_____

_____

_____

_____

_____

♥ *Love* _____

Happy thoughts......

_____

_____

_____

_____

_____

♥ Love_____

Happy thoughts......

_____

_____

_____

_____

_____

♥ Love_____

Happy thoughts......

_____

_____

_____

_____

_____

♥ *Love*

Happy thoughts......

_____

_____

_____

_____

_____

♥ *Love*

Happy thoughts......

_____

_____

_____

_____

_____

 Love

_____

Happy thoughts......

_____

_____

_____

_____

_____

 Love

Happy thoughts......

 Love

Happy thoughts......

 Love

Happy thoughts......

_____

_____

_____

_____

_____

 Love _____

Happy thoughts......

_____

_____

_____

_____

_____

 Love _____

Happy thoughts......

_____

_____

_____

_____

_____

 Love
_____

Happy thoughts......

_____

_____

_____

_____

_____

Love
_____

Happy thoughts......

_____

_____

_____

_____

_____

♥ Love_____

Happy thoughts......

_____

_____

_____

_____

_____

♥ Love_____

Happy thoughts......

_____

_____

_____

_____

_____

♥ *Love*
_____

Happy thoughts......

_____

_____

_____

_____

_____

♥ *Love*
_____

Happy thoughts......

_____

_____

_____

_____

_____

♥ *Love*
_____

Happy thoughts......

_____

_____

_____

_____

_____

♥ *Love*
_____

Gallery of friends

Gallery of friends

Gallery of friends

Gallery of friends

Gallery of friends

Gallery of friends

Gallery of friends

Gallery of friends

Gallery of friends

Gallery of friends

Gallery of friends

Gallery of friends

Gallery of friends

Gallery of friends

Gallery of friends

Gift from	Thank you note sent

Gift from	Thank you note sent